$\mathscr{P}$RESENTED TO

_____

$\mathscr{B}$Y

_____

$\mathscr{D}$ATE

_____

PRAYER of THE DAY

"SPIRITUAL VITAMIN TO ENERGIZE YOUR DAY & NOURISH YOUR SOUL"

TIMOTHY ATUNNISE

HOPE OF VISION PUBLISHING
BRIDGEPORT, CONNECTICUT

PRAYER of THE DAY

"SPIRITUAL VITAMIN TO ENERGIZE YOUR DAY & NOURISH YOUR SOUL"

Timothy Atunnise
Global Vision Ministries Inc.
1096 Bethsaida Road
Riverdale, GA 30296 USA.
information@glovimonline.org
www.glovimonline.org

Hope of Vision Publishing
A division of HOV, LLC.
Bridgeport, CT 06605
Email: Hopeofvision@gmail.com
www.Hopeofvisionpublishing.com

Editor: Elana Simms of Red Pen, LLC

Cover Design: Kaye Coleman
Image by: iStockphoto

For more information about special discounts for bulk purchases contact information@glovimonline.org or visit: www.glovimonline.org.

ISBN 978-0-9818253-9-7
Library of Congress Number: 2009922870

Printed in the United States of America

$\mathcal{D}$EDICATION

This book is dedicated to my wife, Becky,
who stuck it out with me through thick and thin,
through hot and cold, through storm and turbulence.

Thank you for being there,
you are the best, love always.

To every prayer warrior across the globe:
May the Lord give you strength till He comes.

To my Lord Jesus Christ:
Thank you for the mercy and grace you extend
to someone like me.

TABLE OF CONTENT

INTRODUCTION

What is Prayer?

What is prayer? Prayer is our direct line with heaven. Prayer is a communication process that allows us to talk to God! He wants us to communicate with Him, like a person-to-person phone call. Cell phones and other devices have become a necessity to some people in today's society. We have Bluetooth devices, Blackberrys and talking computers! These are means of communication that allow two or more people to interact, discuss and respond to one another. Too many people, prayer seems complicated, but it is simply talking to God.

Prayer is the practice of the presence of God. It is the place where pride is abandoned, hope is lifted and supplication is made. Prayer is the place of admitting our need, of adopting humility and claiming dependence upon God. Prayer is the needful practice of the Christian. Prayer is the exercise of faith and hope. Prayer is the privilege of touching the heart of the Father through the Son of God, Jesus our Lord.

The Bible speaks much of prayer. But, sometimes, too often, we ignore prayer and seek to accomplish in the strength of our own wills those things that we desire to have or happen. For those of us who are too often guilty of this, we need to bow down on our knees, confess our sin, receive God's forgiveness and beg that the will of the Lord be done above our own. God is sovereign and loving and He knows what is best for us and others, even if it doesn't always seem to make the most sense.

So often we come to the Lord with legitimate requests for healing, conversions and needs, and yet the answers we hope for often do not come. We wonder and sometimes doubt. Yet, we persevere and praise God. We pray because we know that God hears us and because we desire to see results. We should pray by faith, trusting God. We should pray consistently, trusting God. We should pray for healing, trusting God. We should pray for others, trusting God. We should pray, period. And when our prayers are answered or are not answered, remember this: If we knew what the Lord knew, we wouldn't change a thing.

Communicating with God changes an individual. In prayer, you are in the presence of God as you lay before Him your complete self in confession and dependence. There is nothing to hide when in quiet supplication, wherein we reach into the deepest part of ourselves and admit our needs and failures. In so doing, our hearts are quieted, pride is stripped and we enjoy the presence of God. James 4:8 says, *"Draw near to God and He will draw near to you."*

I am reminded of another benefit of prayer: Peace. *"Be anxious for nothing, but in everything by prayer and supplication with thanksgiving let your requests be made known to God. And the peace of God, which surpasses all comprehension, shall guard your hearts and your minds in Christ Jesus,"* (Phil. 4:6-7).

I suppose that we can test our prayer life and dependence upon God by the peace, or lack of peace, in our hearts. In all things we are to seek the Lord and in His continued presence peace will surely be our gain.

Prayer is the practice of the presence of God.

DAY 1

PRAYER OF THE DAY

I know I can live a better life, Father God. Let the best you have put in me shine forth, so that everyone around me may see and give glory to your name. I pray in the name of Jesus Christ, with much love and thanksgiving. Amen!

SCRIPTURE OF THE DAY

For brass I will bring gold, and for iron I will bring silver, and for wood brass, and for stones iron: I will also make thy officers peace, and thine exactors righteousness.
-- Isaiah 60:17

TODAY'S WORD OF WISDOM

It takes a lot of courage to release the familiar and seemingly secure, to embrace the new. But there is no real security in what is no longer meaningful. There is more security in the adventurous and exciting. For in movement there is life, and in change there is power.

-- Alan Cohen

DAY 2

PRAYER OF THE DAY

Heavenly Father, prepare me for the blessings you have for me today. Help me to recognize them when they come and give me divine wisdom to manage my blessings. I pray in the name of Jesus Christ, with much love and thanksgiving. Amen!

SCRIPTURE OF THE DAY

Whereas thou hast been forsaken and hated, so that no man went through thee, I will make thee an eternal excellency, a joy of many generations.
-- Isaiah 60:15

TODAY'S WORD OF WISDOM

You can have power over people as long as you don't take everything away from them. But when you've robbed a man of everything, he's no longer in your power.

-- Aleksandri Solzhenitsyn

DAY 3

PRAYER OF THE DAY

In my life today, oh God, let your peace reign. Peace that is beyond human understanding, Let me have peace in every area of my life. I pray in the name of Jesus Christ, with much love and thanksgiving. Amen!

SCRIPTURE OF THE DAY

For I know the thoughts that I think toward you, saith the Lord, thoughts of peace, and not of evil, to give an expected end.
-- Jeremiah 29:11

TODAY'S WORD OF WISDOM

He who is firmly seated in authority soon learns to think security, and not progress, the highest lesson of statecraft.

-- James Russell Lowell

DAY 4

PRAYER OF THE DAY

Today, oh Lord, help me to achieve my goals and fulfill my dreams. I pray in the name of Jesus Christ, with much love and thanksgiving. Amen!

SCRIPTURE OF THE DAY

And they said one to another, Behold, this dreamer cometh. Come now therefore, and let us slay him, and cast him into some pit, and we will say, some evil beast hath devoured him: and we shall see what will become of his dreams.

-- Genesis 37:19-20

TODAY'S WORD OF WISDOM

The key to successful leadership today is influence, not authority.

-- Kenneth Blanchard

DAY 5

PRAYER OF THE DAY

If there is anything in my life that seems impossible, Lord touch it, fix it and make it possible. Impossibility is not in your Word. Do it today and I will give praise to your name. I pray in the name of Jesus Christ, with much love and thanksgiving. Amen!

SCRIPTURE OF THE DAY

But Jesus beheld them, and said unto them, With men this is impossible; but with God all things are possible.

-- Matthew 19:26

TODAY'S WORD OF WISDOM

Always bear in mind that your own resolution to succeed is more important than any other one thing.

-- Abraham Lincoln

DAY 6

PRAYER OF THE DAY

Today, oh Lord, crown me with your favor. Let every situation I find myself in and all business I conduct today favor me. At the end of the day, I shall look back and give glory to your precious name. I pray in the name of Jesus Christ, with much love and thanksgiving. Amen!

SCRIPTURE OF THE DAY

Surely goodness and mercy shall follow me all the days of my life: and I will dwell in the house of the Lord forever.

-- Psalm 23:6

TODAY'S WORD OF WISDOM

If we value independence, if we are disturbed by the growing conformity of knowledge, of values, of attitudes, which our present system induces, then we may wish to set up conditions of learning which make for uniqueness, for self-direction, and for self-initiated learning.

-- Carl Rogers

DAY 7

PRAYER OF THE DAY

A winner never gives up. In the battle of life I shall not give up, no matter how tough the foe. I receive my strength from the Lord and I claim victory over every situation in my life. I pray in the name of Jesus Christ, with much love and thanksgiving. Amen!

SCRIPTURE OF THE DAY

And they overcame him by the blood of the Lamb, and by the word of their testimony; and they loved not their lives unto the death.

-- Revelation 12:11

TODAY'S WORD OF WISDOM

The trick is in what one emphasizes. We either make ourselves miserable, or we make ourselves happy. The amount of work is the same.

-- Carlos Castaneda

DAY 8

PRAYER OF THE DAY

I refuse to be what situations or the economy of this nation dictate people to be. I shall be what I was born to be and I shall fulfill my purpose. I pray in the name of Jesus Christ, with much love and thanksgiving. Amen!

SCRIPTURE OF THE DAY

I the Lord have called thee in righteousness, and will hold thine hand, and will keep thee, and give thee for a covenant of the people, for a light of the Gentiles.

-- Isaiah 42:6

TODAY'S WORD OF WISDOM

To put the world right in order, we must first put the nation in order; to put the nation in order, we must first put the family in order; to put the family in order, we must first cultivate our personal life; we must first set our hearts right.

-- Confucius

DAY 9

PRAYER OF THE DAY

Restore unto me, oh Lord, everything that I have lost through ignorance. Do it today for your name's sake. I pray in the name of Jesus Christ, with much love and thanksgiving. Amen!

SCRIPTURE OF THE DAY

When the Lord turned again the captivity of Zion, we were like them that dream. Then was our mouth filled with laughter, and our tongue with singing: then said they among the heathen, the Lord hath done great things for them.

-- Psalm 126:1-2

TODAY'S WORD OF WISDOM

Small opportunities are often the beginning of great enterprises.

-- Demosthenes

DAY 10

PRAYER OF THE DAY

It's time for me to shine. I refuse to exchange the best that God puts in me with failure. I pray in the name of Jesus Christ, with much love and thanksgiving. Amen!

SCRIPTURE OF THE DAY

Arise, shine; for thy light is come, and the glory of the Lord is risen upon thee. For, behold, the darkness shall cover the earth, and gross darkness the people: but the Lord shall arise upon thee, and his glory shall be seen upon thee.

-- Isaiah 60:1-2

TODAY'S WORD OF WISDOM

Nothing is easier than self-deceit. For what each man wishes, that he also believes to be true.

-- Demosthenes

DAY 11

PRAYER OF THE DAY

I receive the grace of God to overcome every financial problem in my life. I pray in the name of Jesus Christ, with much love and thanksgiving. Amen!

SCRIPTURE OF THE DAY

The Lord is my shepherd; I shall not want.

-- Psalm 23:1

TODAY'S WORD OF WISDOM

The colossal misunderstanding of our time is the assumption that insight will work with people who are unmotivated to change. Communication does not depend on syntax, or eloquence, or rhetoric, or articulation but on the emotional context in which the message is being heard. People can only hear you when they are moving toward you, and they are not likely to when your words are pursuing them. Even the choicest words lose their power when they are used to overpower. Attitudes are the real figures of speech.

-- Edwin Friedman

DAY 12

PRAYER OF THE DAY

I shall be a crown of glory in the hand of the Lord, and a royal diadem in the hand of God. I pray in the name of Jesus Christ, with much love and thanksgiving. Amen!

SCRIPTURE OF THE DAY

Thou shalt also be a crown of glory in the hand of the Lord, and a royal diadem in the hand of thy God.

-- Isaiah 62:3

TODAY'S WORD OF WISDOM

The thing always happens that you really believe in; and the belief in a thing makes it happen.

-- **Frank Lloyd Wright**

DAY 13

PRAYER OF THE DAY

Today, oh Lord, speak restoration to every barren (unfruitful) area of my life and let my life bring forth good things. I pray in the name of Jesus Christ, with much love and thanksgiving. Amen!

SCRIPTURE OF THE DAY

And God blessed them, and God said unto them, Be fruitful, and multiply, and replenish the earth, and subdue it: and have dominion over the fish of the sea, and over the fowl of the air, and over every living thing that moveth upon the earth.

-- Genesis 1:28

TODAY'S WORD OF WISDOM

The basic thing is that everyone wants happiness; no one wants suffering. And happiness mainly comes from our own attitude, rather than from external factors. If your own mental attitude is correct, even if you remain in a hostile atmosphere, you feel happy.

-- Unknown

DAY 14

PRAYER OF THE DAY

You are the great provider. Today, oh Lord, provide for all my physical, spiritual, material and financial needs according to your Word. I pray in the name of Jesus Christ, with much love and thanksgiving. Amen!

SCRIPTURE OF THE DAY

But my God shall supply all your need according to his riches in glory by Christ Jesus.

-- Philippians 4:19

TODAY'S WORD OF WISDOM

When one door of happiness closes, another opens; but often we look so long at the closed door that we do not see the one which has been opened for us.

-- Helen Keller

DAY 15

PRAYER OF THE DAY

I shall be like a tree planted by streams of water. My life shall yield fruits in season and my leaf shall not wither. Whatever I do shall prosper. I pray in the name of Jesus Christ, with much love and thanksgiving. Amen!

SCRIPTURE OF THE DAY

And he shall be like a tree planted by the rivers of water, that bringeth forth his fruit in his season; his leaf also shall not wither; and whatsoever he doeth shall prosper.

-- Psalm 1:3

TODAY'S WORD OF WISDOM

Thought is the sculptor who can create the person you want to be.

-- Henry David Thoreau

DAY 16

PRAYER OF THE DAY

Remember me today, oh my God, for good. I pray in the name of Jesus Christ, with much love and thanksgiving. Amen!

SCRIPTURE OF THE DAY

Remember me, O my God, concerning this, and wipe not out my good deeds that I have done for the house of my God, and for the offices thereof.

-- Nehemiah 13:14

TODAY'S WORD OF WISDOM

If you think you can, you can. And if you think you can't, you're right.

-- Henry Ford

DAY 17

PRAYER OF THE DAY

Today, oh Lord, do in my life what you alone can do. I pray in the name of Jesus Christ, with much love and thanksgiving. Amen!

SCRIPTURE OF THE DAY

For with God nothing shall be impossible.

-- Luke 1:37

TODAY'S WORD OF WISDOM

The most successful people are those who are good at plan B.

-- James Yorke

DAY 18

PRAYER OF THE DAY

Today, oh Lord, let there be a positive change in my life; change that everyone around me will notice and rejoice with me. I pray in the name of Jesus Christ, with much love and thanksgiving. Amen!

SCRIPTURE OF THE DAY

And God said, Let there be light: and there was light. And God saw the light, that it was good: and God divided the light from the darkness.

-- Genesis 1:3-4

TODAY'S WORD OF WISDOM

The truth is that our finest moments are most likely to occur when we are feeling deeply uncomfortable, unhappy, or unfulfilled. For it is only in such moments, propelled by our discomfort, that we are likely to step out of our ruts and start searching for different ways or true answers.

-- Scott Peck

DAY 19

PRAYER OF THE DAY

With my mouth, oh Lord, I speak success unto every good thing I lay my hands upon today. I pray in the name of Jesus Christ, with much love and thanksgiving. Amen!

SCRIPTURE OF THE DAY

Death and life are in the power of the tongue: and they that love it shall eat the fruit thereof.

-- Proverbs 18:21

TODAY'S WORD OF WISDOM

If you are distressed by anything external, the pain is not due to the thing itself, but to your estimate of it; and this you have the power to revoke at any moment.

-- Marcus Aurelius

DAY 20

PRAYER OF THE DAY

Today, oh Lord, let the heaven of blessings and prosperity open unto me, and I will enjoy the blessings of heaven. I pray in the name of Jesus Christ, with much love and thanksgiving. Amen!

SCRIPTURE OF THE DAY

...... Test me in this," says the LORD Almighty, "and see if I will not throw open the floodgates of heaven and pour out so much blessing that there will not be room enough to store it.

-- Malachi 3:10 TNIV

TODAY'S WORD OF WISDOM

You really *can* change the world if you care enough.

-- Marian Edelman

DAY 21

PRAYER OF THE DAY

Today, oh Lord, I shall not waste my time. I shall be in the right place, at the right time, and meet with the right people, to do the right things, so, at the end of the day, my life shall bring forth better results. I pray in the name of Jesus Christ, with much love and thanksgiving. Amen!

SCRIPTURE OF THE DAY

There is time for everything, and a season for every activity under the heavens.

-- Ecclesiastes 3:1

TODAY'S WORD OF WISDOM

And as we let our own light shine, we unconsciously give other people permission to do the same. As we are liberated from our fear, our presence automatically liberates others.

-- Marianne Williamson

DAY 22

PRAYER OF THE DAY

Father and Lord, I believe in miracles. Send your miracles into my life that will change it for the better. I pray in the name of Jesus Christ, with much love and thanksgiving. Amen!

SCRIPTURE OF THE DAY

Jesus saith unto him, Rise, take up thy bed, and walk. And immediately the man was made whole, and took up his bed, and walked: and on the same day was the sabbath.

-- John 5:8-9

TODAY'S WORD OF WISDOM

The greatest part of our happiness depends on our dispositions, not our circumstances.

-- Martha Washington

DAY 23

PRAYER OF THE DAY

Today, oh Lord, help me to forgive those who have offended and hurt me. Give me grace and strength to look beyond what they have done to me. I pray in the name of Jesus Christ, with much love and thanksgiving. Amen!

SCRIPTURE OF THE DAY

After this manner therefore pray ye: Our Father which art in heaven, hallowed be thy name. Thy kingdom come. Thy will be done in earth, as it is in heaven. Give us this day our daily bread. And forgive us our trespasses, as we forgive those who trespass against us.

-- Matthew 6:9-12

TODAY'S WORD OF WISDOM

To succeed, we must first believe that we can.

-- Michael Korda

DAY 24

PRAYER OF THE DAY

Today, oh Lord, send me a good and special gift that will make my life a testimony to the world. I pray in the name of Jesus Christ, with much love and thanksgiving. Amen!

SCRIPTURE OF THE DAY

Every good gift and every perfect gift is from above, and cometh down from the Father of lights, with whom is no variableness, neither shadow of turning.

-- James 1:17

TODAY'S WORD OF WISDOM

Life is a train of moods like a string of beads; and as we pass through them they prove to be many colored lenses, which paint the world their own hue, and each shows us only what lies in its own focus.

-- **Ralph Emerson**

DAY 25

PRAYER OF THE DAY

Today, oh Lord, touch every area of my life that I don't like to discuss because of pain and shame. Heal my pain and take away my shame for there is absolutely nothing you cannot do. I pray in the name of Jesus Christ, with much love and thanksgiving. Amen!

SCRIPTURE OF THE DAY

Behold, I am the Lord, the God of all flesh: is there any thing too hard for me?

-- Jeremiah 32:27

TODAY'S WORD OF WISDOM

Sooner or later, those who win are those who think they can.

-- Richard Bach

DAY 26

PRAYER OF THE DAY

With the authority and power given to me in Christ Jesus, I break every curse upon my life designed to make me a loser in any area of life. I pray in the name of Jesus Christ, with much love and thanksgiving. Amen!

SCRIPTURE OF THE DAY

Then He called his twelve disciples together, and gave them power and authority over all devils, and to cure diseases. And he sent them to preach the kingdom of God, and to heal the sick.

-- Luke 9:1-2

TODAY'S WORD OF WISDOM

Peace is not the absence of war; it is a virtue, a state of mind; a disposition for benevolence, confidence; and justice.

-- Baruch Spinoza

DAY 27

PRAYER OF THE DAY

Today, oh Lord, I refuse to cooperate with the power of the enemy intended to rob me of my blessings. I pray in the name of Jesus Christ, with much love and thanksgiving. Amen!

SCRIPTURE OF THE DAY

Behold, I come quickly: hold that fast which thou hast, that no man take thy crown.

-- Revelation 3:11

TODAY'S WORD OF WISDOM

Opportunity is missed by most because it is dressed in overalls and looks like work.

-- Thomas Edison

DAY 28

PRAYER OF THE DAY

For the remaining days of this year, oh Lord, let my outgoing and incoming be according to your will. Protect me from any danger. I pray in the name of Jesus Christ, with much love and thanksgiving. Amen!

SCRIPTURE OF THE DAY

A thousand shall fall at thy side, and ten thousand at thy right hand; but it shall not come nigh thee. Only with thine eyes shalt thou behold and see the reward of the wicked. Because thou hast made the Lord, which is my refuge, even the most High, thy habitation. There shall no evil befall thee, neither shall any plague come nigh thy dwelling

-- Psalm 91:7-10

TODAY'S WORD OF WISDOM

The greatest discovery of any generation is that a human being can alter his life by altering his attitude.

-- William James

DAY 29

PRAYER OF THE DAY

Father and Lord, let your will for my life be established and let the wish of the enemy fail. I pray in the name of Jesus Christ, with much love and thanksgiving. Amen!

SCRIPTURE OF THE DAY

After this manner therefore pray ye: Our Father which art in heaven, hallowed be thy name. Thy kingdom come. Thy will be done in earth, as it is in heaven.

-- Matthew 6:9-10

TODAY'S WORD OF WISDOM

The greatest discovery of our generation is that human beings can alter their lives by altering their attitudes of mind. As you think, so shall you be.

-- William James

DAY 30

PRAYER OF THE DAY

Father God, in any area that I have made mistakes in life, have mercy on me and give me a second chance. I pray in the name of Jesus Christ, with much love and thanksgiving. Amen!

SCRIPTURE OF THE DAY

And He said, I will make all my goodness pass before thee, and I will proclaim the name of the Lord before thee; and will be gracious to whom I will be gracious, and will show mercy on whom I will show mercy.

-- Exodus 33:19

TODAY'S WORD OF WISDOM

The world is a dangerous place, not because of those who do evil, but because of those who look on and do nothing.

-- Albert Einstein

DAY 31

PRAYER OF THE DAY

Today, oh Lord, give me strength to overcome every obstacle on my way to greater achievements. I pray in the name of Jesus Christ, with much love and thanksgiving. Amen!

SCRIPTURE OF THE DAY

He that hath an ear, let him hear what the Spirit saith unto the churches; To him that overcometh will I give to eat of the hidden manna, and will give him a white stone, and in the stone a new name written, which no man knoweth saving he that receiveth it.

-- Revelation 2:17

TODAY'S WORD OF WISDOM

Dreams pass into the reality of action. From the actions stems the dream again; and this interdependence produces the highest form of living.

-- Anais Nin

DAY 32

PRAYER OF THE DAY

Help me, oh Lord, to identify and deal with any weakness in me that can hinder my progress. I pray in the name of Jesus Christ, with much love and thanksgiving. Amen!

SCRIPTURE OF THE DAY

I can do all things through Christ which strengtheneth me.

-- Philippians 4:13

TODAY'S WORD OF WISDOM

Knowing others is intelligence; knowing yourself is true wisdom. Mastering others is strength; mastering yourself is true power.

-- Unknown

DAY 33

PRAYER OF THE DAY

Today, oh Lord, I receive anointing to excel above my contemporaries. I pray in the name of Jesus Christ, with much love and thanksgiving. Amen!

SCRIPTURE OF THE DAY

And the Lord shall make thee the head, and not the tail; and thou shalt be above only, and thou shalt not be beneath; if that thou hearken unto the commandments of the Lord thy God, which I command thee this day, to observe and to do them.

-- Deuteronomy 28:13

TODAY'S WORD OF WISDOM

Good friends are like stars. You don't always see them, but you know they are always there.

--Unknown

DAY 34

PRAYER OF THE DAY

Today, oh Lord, bless my outgoing and my incoming. Bless everything I touch and everything I do. I pray in the name of Jesus Christ, Amen!

SCRIPTURE OF THE DAY

Blessed shall thou be when thou comest in, and blessed shalt thou be when thou goest out.

-- Deuteronomy 28:6.

TODAY'S WORD OF WISDOM

Wise men speak because they have something to say; Fools because they have to say something.

-- Plato

DAY 35

PRAYER OF THE DAY

Father and Lord, let the blood of Jesus be released on my behalf
and let it speak against every stubborn mountain in my life. I pray
in the name of Jesus Christ, with much love and thanksgiving.
Amen!

SCRIPTURE OF THE DAY

And Jesus the mediator of the new covenant, and to the blood of
sprinkling, that speaketh better things than that of Abel.

-- Hebrews 12:24.

TODAY'S WORD OF WISDOM

To accomplish great things, we must not only act, but also dream;
not only plan, but also believe.

-- Anatole France

DAY 36

PRAYER OF THE DAY

Father and Lord, let all problems that originate from my past mistakes be converted to miracles and promotion. I pray in the name of Jesus Christ, with much love and thanksgiving. Amen!

SCRIPTURE OF THE DAY

Who art thou, O great mountain? before Zerubbabel thou shalt become a plain: and he shall bring forth the headstone thereof with shouting, crying, Grace, grace unto it.

--Zechariah 4:7

TODAY'S WORD OF WISDOM

One act of beneficence, one act of real usefulness, is worth all the abstract sentiment in the world.

-- Ann Radcliffe

DAY 37

PRAYER OF THE DAY

Father and Lord, I just want to thank you for your good hands upon me and everything you are doing in my life. I pray in the name of Jesus Christ, with much love and thanksgiving. Amen!

SCRIPTURE OF THE DAY

Unto thee, O God, do we give thanks, unto thee do we give thanks: for that thy name is near thy wondrous works declare.

--Psalm 75:1

TODAY'S WORD OF WISDOM

How we spend our days is, of course, how we spend our lives.

-- **Annie Dillard**

DAY 38

PRAYER OF THE DAY

Almighty God, who quickens the dead and calls those things that be not as if they are, release upon me today anointing to succeed in every area of life. I pray in the name of Jesus Christ, with much love and thanksgiving. Amen!

SCRIPTURE OF THE DAY

But if the Spirit of Him that raised up Jesus from the dead dwelleth in you, He that raised up Christ from the dead shall also quicken your mortal bodies by His Spirit that dwells in you.

-- Romans 8:11

TODAY'S WORD OF WISDOM

Moral excellence comes about as a result of habit. We become just by doing just acts, temperate by doing temperate acts, brave by doing brave acts.

-- **Aristotle**

DAY 39

PRAYER OF THE DAY

The terror of the night shall not be my portion and the arrow of the day shall not be my lot, for my God will protect my household and me from any danger. I pray in the name of Jesus Christ, with much love and thanksgiving. Amen!

SCRIPTURE OF THE DAY

Thou shalt not be afraid for the terror by the night; nor for the arrow that flieth by day; nor for the pestilence that walketh in darkness; nor for the destruction that wasteth at noonday.

--Psalm 91:5-6

TODAY'S WORD OF WISDOM

Apathy can be overcome by enthusiasm, and enthusiasm can only be aroused by two things: first, an ideal, with takes the imagination by storm, and second, a definite intelligible plan for carrying that ideal into practice.

--Arnold Toynbee

DAY 40

PRAYER OF THE DAY

Father and Lord, I just want to say "THANK YOU" for giving me many reasons to be thankful. I pray in the name of Jesus Christ, with much love and thanksgiving. Amen!

SCRIPTURE OF THE DAY

Bless the Lord, O my soul: and all that is within me, bless his holy name. Bless the Lord, O my soul, and forget not all his benefits: Who forgiveth all thine iniquities; who healeth all thy diseases; who redeemeth thy life from destruction; who crowneth thee with lovingkindness and tender mercies; who satisfieth thy mouth with good things; so that thy youth is renewed like the eagle's.

--Psalm 103:1-5

TODAY'S WORD OF WISDOM

The well bred contradict other people. The wise contradict themselves.

-- Oscar Wilde

DAY 41

PRAYER OF THE DAY

A touch from the Lord changes things forever. Today, oh Lord, let every work of my hands receive a divine touch from you. I pray in the name of Jesus Christ, with much love and thanksgiving. Amen!

SCRIPTURE OF THE DAY

Beloved, I wish above all things that thou mayest prosper and be in health even as thy soul prospereth.

--3 John 1:2

TODAY'S WORD OF WISDOM

Action may not always bring happiness, but there is no happiness without action.

--Benjamin Disraeli

DAY 42

PRAYER OF THE DAY

Father God, grant me peace of mind and let my fear go away. I pray in the name of Jesus Christ, with much love and thanksgiving. Amen!

SCRIPTURE OF THE DAY

The Lord is my light and my salvation; whom shall I fear? the Lord is the strength of my life; of whom shall I be afraid?

--Psalm 27:1

TODAY'S WORD OF WISDOM

You can judge your age by the amount of pain you feel when you come in contact with a new idea.

--Pearl S. Buck

DAY 43

PRAYER OF THE DAY

Father and Lord, let my expected breakthroughs manifest before this year runs to an end. I pray in the name of Jesus Christ, with much love and thanksgiving. Amen!

SCRIPTURE OF THE DAY

The Lord hath been mindful of us: he will bless us; he will bless the house of Israel; he will bless the house of Aaron. He will bless them that fear the Lord, both small and great. The Lord shall increase you more and more, you and your children. Ye are blessed of the Lord which made heaven and earth. The heaven, even the heavens, are the Lord's: but the earth hath he given to the children of men.

--Psalm 115:12-16

TODAY'S WORD OF WISDOM

You cannot make yourself feel something you do not feel, but you can make yourself do right in spite of your feelings.

--Pearl S. Buck

DAY 44

PRAYER OF THE DAY

Father God, your Word says nothing is impossible for you. Every stubborn situation in my life that seems unfixable, touch with your mighty hands and fix them today for your name's sake. I pray in the name of Jesus Christ, with much love and thanksgiving. Amen!

SCRIPTURE OF THE DAY

Behold, I am the Lord, the God of all flesh: is there anything too hard for me?.

--Jeremiah 32:27

TODAY'S WORD OF WISDOM

It is always easier to believe than to deny. Our minds are naturally affirmative.

--John Burroughs

DAY 45

PRAYER OF THE DAY

Make my life, oh God, your dwelling place. Build your throne in my heart and cover me with your glory. Let everyone see Christ in me, the hope of glory. I pray in the name of Jesus Christ, with much love and thanksgiving. Amen!

SCRIPTURE OF THE DAY

But we all, with open face beholding as in a glass the glory of the Lord, are changed into the same image from glory to glory, even as by the Spirit of the Lord.

--2 Corinthians 3:18

TODAY'S WORD OF WISDOM

The test of courage comes when we are in the minority. The test of tolerance comes when we are in the majority.

--Ralph Sockman

DAY 46

PRAYER OF THE DAY

Let your good hands, oh Lord, guide and protect me from every danger; I shall go out and come in safely and no evil shall come near my dwelling. I pray in the name of Jesus Christ, with much love and thanksgiving. Amen!

SCRIPTURE OF THE DAY

There shall no evil befall thee, neither shall any plague come near thy dwelling. For he shall give his angels charge over thee, to keep thee in all thy ways. They shall bear thee up in their hands, lest thou dash thy foot against a stone.

--Psalm 91:10-12

TODAY'S WORD OF WISDOM

It is only through your conscious mind that you can reach the subconscious. Your conscious mind is the porter at the door, the watchman at the gate. It is to the conscious mind that the subconscious looks for all its impressions.

--Robert Collier

DAY 47

PRAYER OF THE DAY

Deliver me, oh God, with your right hand of righteousness from all inherited and self-inflicted curses. As from today, I begin to live a better, meaningful and productive life. I pray in the name of Jesus Christ, with much love and thanksgiving. Amen!

SCRIPTURE OF THE DAY

Christ hath redeemed us from the curse of the law, being made a curse for us: for it is written, Cursed is every one that hangeth on a tree: That the blessing of Abraham might come on the Gentiles through Jesus Christ; that we might receive the promise of the Spirit through faith.

--Galatians 3:13-14

TODAY'S WORD OF WISDOM

The major block to compassion is the judgment in our minds. Judgment is the mind's primary tool of separation.

--Diane Berke

DAY 48

PRAYER OF THE DAY

Father and Lord, let all blessings, breakthroughs, good health, miracles, victory, promotions, business opportunities and heart's desires that I have lost be restored back to me today. Give me another chance to enjoy blessings that you designed for me. I pray in the name of Jesus Christ, with much love and thanksgiving.
Amen!

SCRIPTURE OF THE DAY

And God blessed them, and God said unto them, Be fruitful, and multiply, and replenish the earth, and subdue it: and have dominion over the fish of the sea, and over the fowl of the air, and over every living thing that moveth upon the earth.

--Genesis 1:28

TODAY'S WORD OF WISDOM

The future belongs to those who give the next generation reason for hope.

-- Pierre Teilhard de Chardin

DAY 49

PRAYER OF THE DAY

I draw a circle of the blood of Jesus around me. I draw the blood line of protection around my property. I overcome you Satan by the blood of the Lamb. You cannot put any sickness on me because I am redeemed by the blood of the Lamb. I pray in the name of Jesus Christ, with much love and thanksgiving. Amen!

SCRIPTURE OF THE DAY

And they overcame him by the blood of the Lamb, and by the word of their testimony; and they loved not their lives unto the death.

--Revelation 12:11

TODAY'S WORD OF WISDOM

Giving frees us from the familiar territory of our own needs by opening our mind to the unexplained worlds occupied by the needs of others.

--Barbara Bush

DAY 50

PRAYER OF THE DAY

Today, oh Lord, I reclaim all my goods presently residing in wrong hands, even with dividends. I pray in the name of Jesus Christ, with much love and thanksgiving. Amen!

SCRIPTURE OF THE DAY

And the ark of the Lord was in the country of the Philistines seven months. And the Philistines called the priests and the diviners, saying, what shall we do to the ark of the Lord? Tell us wherewith we shall send it to his place. And they said if ye send away the ark of the God of Israel, send it not empty; but in any wise return him a trespass offering: then ye shall be healed, and it shall be known to you why his hand is not removed from you.

--1 Samuel 6:1-3

TODAY'S WORD OF WISDOM

Every time we love, every time we give, it's Christmas.

--Dale Evans

DAY 51

PRAYER OF THE DAY

Oh Lord, establish me in every good work. I pray in the name of
Jesus Christ, with much love and thanksgiving. Amen!

SCRIPTURE OF THE DAY

But I say unto you, Love your enemies, bless them that curse you,
do good to them that hate you, and pray for them that despitefully
use you, and persecute you; That ye may be the children of your
Father which is in heaven: for he maketh his sun to rise on the evil
and on the good, and sendeth rain on the just and on the unjust.

--Matthew 5:44-45

TODAY'S WORD OF WISDOM

Generosity during life is a very different thing from generosity in
the hour of death; one proceeds from genuine liberality and
benevolence, the other from pride or fear.

--Horace Mann

DAY 52

PRAYER OF THE DAY

When I woke up this morning, Lord, I knew you gave me another chance to live for a purpose. Help me to fulfill my purpose before the day is over. I pray in the name of Jesus Christ, with much love and thanksgiving. Amen!

SCRIPTURE OF THE DAY

In whom also we have obtained an inheritance, being predestinated according to the purpose of him who worketh all things after the counsel of his own will.

--Ephesians 1:11

TODAY'S WORD OF WISDOM

Think of giving not as a duty but as a privilege.

--John D Rockefeller Jr.

DAY 53

PRAYER OF THE DAY

Life's journey is tough and rough, but I will wait upon you, oh
Lord, to renew my strength, I shall mount up with wings as eagles;
I shall run and not be weary; I shall walk and not faint. I pray in
the name of Jesus Christ, with much love and thanksgiving. Amen!

SCRIPTURE OF THE DAY

He giveth power to the faint; and to them that have no might he
increaseth strength. Even the youths shall faint and be weary, and
the young men shall utterly fail: But they that wait upon the Lord
shall renew their strength; they shall mount up with wings as
eagles; they shall run, and not be weary; and they shall walk, and
not faint.

--Isaiah 40:29-31

TODAY'S WORD OF WISDOM

One isn't necessarily born with courage, but one is born with
potential. Without courage, we cannot practice any other virtue
with consistency. We can't be kind, true, merciful, generous, or
honest.

--Maya Angelou

DAY 54

PRAYER OF THE DAY

Let the spirit of excellence come upon me today, oh Lord, and make me a joy of my generation. I pray in the name of Jesus Christ, with much love and thanksgiving. Amen!

SCRIPTURE OF THE DAY

Whereas thou has been forsaken and hated, so that no man went through thee, I will make thee an eternal excellency, a joy of many generations.

--Isaiah 60:15

TODAY'S WORD OF WISDOM

Giving presents is a talent; to know what a person wants, to know when and how to get it, to give it lovingly and well. Unless a character possesses this talent there is no moment more annihilating to ease than that in which a present is received and given.

--Pamela Glenconner

DAY 55

PRAYER OF THE DAY

Let your Word dwell in me, oh Lord, for I need you now more than never. I pray in the name of Jesus Christ, with much love and thanksgiving. Amen!

SCRIPTURE OF THE DAY

I have declared my ways, and thou heardest me: teach me thy statutes. Make me to understand the way of thy precepts; so shall I talk of thy wondrous works. My soul melteth for heaviness: strengthen thou me according to thy word.

--Psalm 119:26-28

TODAY'S WORD OF WISDOM

There is a wonderful mythical law of nature that the three things we crave most in life -- happiness, freedom, and peace of mind -- are always attained by giving them to someone else.

--Peyton Conway March

DAY 56

PRAYER OF THE DAY

Today, oh Lord, let me find your favor in whatever I do and wherever I go. I pray in the name of Jesus Christ, with much love and thanksgiving. Amen!

SCRIPTURE OF THE DAY

For thou, LORD, wilt bless the righteous; with favour wilt thou compass him as with a shield.

--Psalm 5:12

TODAY'S WORD OF WISDOM

There is no beautifier of complexion, or form, or behavior, like the wish to scatter joy and not pain around us. 'Tis good to give a stranger a meal, or a night's lodging. 'Tis better to be hospitable to his good meaning and thought, and give courage to a companion. We must be as courteous to a man as we are to a picture, which we are willing to give the advantage of a good light.

--Ralph Waldo Emerson

DAY 57

PRAYER OF THE DAY

Today, oh Lord, bless my incoming and outgoing. Rain upon me the blessings of heaven. I pray in the name of Jesus Christ, with much love and thanksgiving. Amen!

SCRIPTURE OF THE DAY

The young lions do lack, and suffer hunger: but they that seek the Lord shall not want any good thing.

--Psalm 34:10

TODAY'S WORD OF WISDOM

Money is like manure; it's not worth a thing unless it's spread around encouraging young things to grow.

--Thornton Wilder

DAY 58

PRAYER OF THE DAY

You promised me, oh Lord, that you will always be with me, no matter how tough the road, no matter the situation, I will not quit nor give up because you are on my side and my victory is sure. I pray in the name of Jesus Christ, with much love and thanksgiving. Amen!

SCRIPTURE OF THE DAY

When thou passeth through the waters, I will be with thee; and through the rivers, they shall not overflow thee: when thou walkest through the fire, thou shall not be burned; neither shall the flame kindle upon thee.

--Isaiah 43:2

TODAY'S WORD OF WISDOM

The habit of giving only enhances the desire to give.

--Walt Whitman

DAY 59

PRAYER OF THE DAY

Lord, your Word says life and death are in the power of my
tongue. Today I speak solutions to every situation around me, and
peace be still to every storm. I pray in the name of Jesus Christ,
with much love and thanksgiving. Amen!

SCRIPTURE OF THE DAY

Death and life are in the power of the tongue: and they that love it
shall it eat the fruit thereof.

--Proverbs 18:21.

TODAY'S WORD OF WISDOM

You make a living by what you get. You make a life by what you
give.

--Winston Churchill

DAY 60

PRAYER OF THE DAY

Lord, your Word says, God is not a man, that he should lie. You promised me many things. Today, oh Lord, remember your promises to fulfill them before this year passes away, no matter how impossible it seems to me. I pray in the name of Jesus Christ, with much love and thanksgiving. Amen!

SCRIPTURE OF THE DAY

God is not a man, that he should lie; neither the son of man, that he should repent: hath he said, and shall he not do it? or hath he spoken, and shall he not make it good?.

--Numbers 23:19.

TODAY'S WORD OF WISDOM

Setting an example is not the main means of influencing another, it is the only means.

--Albert Einstein

DAY 61

PRAYER OF THE DAY

Today, oh Lord, speak into my life, and let your voice give me comfort, peace and joy. I pray in the name of Jesus Christ, with much love and thanksgiving. Amen!

SCRIPTURE OF THE DAY

The voice of the Lord is upon many waters: the God of glory thundereth: the Lord is upon many waters. The voice of the Lord is powerful; the voice of the Lord is full of majesty.

--Psalm 29:3-4

TODAY'S WORD OF WISDOM

The right to be heard does not automatically include the right to be taken seriously.

--Hubert Humphrey

DAY 62

PRAYER OF THE DAY

Lord, your Word says, you'll show mercy on whom you'll show mercy. Have mercy on me, oh Lord, according to your Word. I pray in the name of Jesus Christ, with much love and thanksgiving. Amen!

SCRIPTURE OF THE DAY

And he said, I will make all my goodness pass before thee, and I will proclaim the name of the Lord before thee; and will be gracious to whom I will be gracious, and will shew mercy on whom I will shew mercy.

--Exodus 33:19

TODAY'S WORD OF WISDOM

Love measures our stature: the more we love, the bigger we are. There is no smaller package in all the world than that of a man all wrapped up in himself.

--William Sloane Coffin Jr.

DAY 63

PRAYER OF THE DAY

Anything in me that hinders the fulfillment of your promises in my life, Father God, take it away from me and fulfill your promises in my life. I pray in the name of Jesus Christ, with much love and thanksgiving. Amen!

SCRIPTURE OF THE DAY

For I know the thoughts that I think toward you, saith the Lord, thoughts of peace, and not of evil, to give you an expected end.

--Jeremiah 29:11

TODAY'S WORD OF WISDOM

Nobody can be so amusingly arrogant as a young man who has just discovered an old idea and thinks it is his own.

--Sydney J Harris

DAY 64

PRAYER OF THE DAY

Lord, you are a present help in time of trouble, therefore I will not
be afraid; no matter how rough the road, no matter how tough the
journey, because you've promised me safe arrival. I believe it and I
claim it. I pray in the name of Jesus Christ, with much love and
thanksgiving. Amen!

SCRIPTURE OF THE DAY

God is our refuge and strength, a very present help in trouble.
Therefore will not we fear, though the earth be removed, and
though the mountains be carried into the midst of the sea; though
the waters thereof roar and be troubled, though the mountains
shake with the swelling thereof.

--Psalm 46:1-3

TODAY'S WORD OF WISDOM

The demand to be loved is the greatest of all arrogant
presumptions.

--Friedrich Nietzsche

DAY 65

PRAYER OF THE DAY

Lord, let all my efforts today bring me success and fruitfulness. I pray in the name of Jesus Christ, with much love and thanksgiving. Amen!

SCRIPTURE OF THE DAY

Blessed shall be the fruit of thy body, and the fruit of thy ground, and the fruit of thy cattle, the increase of thy kine, and the flocks of thy sheep. Blessed shall be thy basket and thy store.

--Deuteronomy 28:4-5

TODAY'S WORD OF WISDOM

The true means of being misled is to believe oneself is finer than the others.

-- **Duc De La Rochefoucauld**

DAY 66

PRAYER OF THE DAY

Lord, protect me from falling into temptation, and deliver me from evil. I pray in the name of Jesus Christ, with much love and thanksgiving. Amen!

SCRIPTURE OF THE DAY

And lead us not into temptation, but deliver us from evil: For thine is the kingdom, and the power, and the glory, forever. Amen.

--Matthew 6:13

TODAY'S WORD OF WISDOM

Dreams pass into the reality of action. From the actions stems the dream again; and this interdependence produces the highest form of living.

--Anais Nin

DAY 67

PRAYER OF THE DAY

I am crying and looking unto you, oh Lord. Let my voice be heard, grant my requests and give me the desires of my heart. I pray in the name of Jesus Christ, with much love and thanksgiving. Amen!

SCRIPTURE OF THE DAY

Call unto me, and I will answer thee, and show thee great and mighty things, which thou knowest not.

--Jeremiah 33:3

TODAY'S WORD OF WISDOM

The dream was always running ahead of me. To catch up, to live for a moment in unison with it, that was the miracle.

--Anais Nin

DAY 68

PRAYER OF THE DAY

Release upon me today, oh Lord, blessings that will make me forget my sorrow, shame, reproach and pain; and restore my happiness. I pray in the name of Jesus Christ, with much love and thanksgiving. Amen!

SCRIPTURE OF THE DAY

Fear not; for thou shalt not be ashamed: neither be thou confounded; for thou shalt not be put to shame: for thou shalt forget the shame of thy youth, and shalt not remember the reproach of thy widowhood any more.

--Isaiah 54:4

TODAY'S WORD OF WISDOM

Dreams are necessary to life.

--Anais Nin

DAY 69

PRAYER OF THE DAY

Let fire of God consume anything in me that is not of God, and let me live a pure and fulfilling life. I pray in the name of Jesus Christ, with much love and thanksgiving. Amen!

SCRIPTURE OF THE DAY

Wherefore we receiving a kingdom which cannot be moved, let us have grace, whereby we may serve God acceptably with reverence and godly fear: For our God is a consuming fire.

--Hebrews 12:28-29

TODAY'S WORD OF WISDOM

To accomplish great things, we must not only act, but also dream; not only plan, but also believe.

--Anatole France

DAY 70

PRAYER OF THE DAY

Grant unto me, oh God, the mind of Christ: A forgiving spirit, tolerance, genuine repentance, understanding, submission, humility, brokenness, watchfulness and the mind to commit others better than myself. I pray in the name of Jesus Christ, with much love and thanksgiving. Amen!

SCRIPTURE OF THE DAY

I beseech you therefore, brethren, by the mercies of God, that ye present your bodies a living sacrifice, holy, acceptable unto God, which is your reasonable service. And be not conformed to this world: but be ye transformed by the renewing of your mind, that ye may prove what is that good, and acceptable, and perfect, will of God.

--Romans 12:1-2

TODAY'S WORD OF WISDOM

Your vision will become clear only when you look into your heart. Who looks outside, dreams. Who looks inside, awakens.

--Carl Jung

DAY 71

PRAYER OF THE DAY

Connect me, oh God, with people that have the right information to lead me to my promise land. I pray in the name of Jesus Christ, with much love and thanksgiving. Amen!

SCRIPTURE OF THE DAY

Lift up thine eyes round about, and see: all they gather themselves together, they come to thee: thy sons shall come from far, and thy daughters shall be nursed at thy side. Then thou shalt see, and flow together, and thine heart shall fear, and be enlarged; because the abundance of the sea shall be converted unto thee, the forces of the Gentiles shall come unto thee.

--Isaiah 60:4-5

TODAY'S WORD OF WISDOM

Nothing happens unless first we dream.

--Carl Sandburg

DAY 72

PRAYER OF THE DAY

Father God, thank you for giving me your only son as a gift to die for me. Let me be a shining light for you, and let me be a joy to you always. I pray in the name of Jesus Christ, with much love and thanksgiving. Amen!

SCRIPTURE OF THE DAY

For God so loved the world, that he gave his only begotten Son, that whosoever believeth in him should not perish, but have everlasting life.

--John 3:16

TODAY'S WORD OF WISDOM

When we are dreaming alone it is only a dream. When we are dreaming with others, it is the beginning of reality.

--Dom Helder Camara

DAY 73

PRAYER OF THE DAY

Lord, is there any area in my life over which I have not given you total control? Forgive me today, lead me, direct me and take total control of my life. I pray in the name of Jesus Christ, with much love and thanksgiving. Amen!

SCRIPTURE OF THE DAY

Thy word is a lamp unto my feet, and a light unto my path. I have sworn, and I will perform it, that I will keep thy righteous judgments.

--Psalm 119:105-106

TODAY'S WORD OF WISDOM

The work goes on, the cause endures, the hope still lives and the dreams shall never die.

--Edward Kennedy

DAY 74

PRAYER OF THE DAY

Today, oh Lord, I trade my sorrow, pain, disappointment, failure and shame for the joy of the Lord. Let the immeasurable joy of the Lord be my strength and help me to forget all my painful experiences. I pray in the name of Jesus Christ, with much love and thanksgiving. Amen!

SCRIPTURE OF THE DAY

Then he said unto them, Go your way, eat the fat, and drink the sweet, and send portions unto them for whom nothing is prepared: for this day is holy unto our Lord: neither be ye sorry; for the joy of the Lord is your strength.

--Nehemiah 8:10

TODAY'S WORD OF WISDOM

The inability to open up to hope is what blocks trust, and blocked trust is the reason for blighted dreams.

--Elizabeth Gilbert

DAY 75

PRAYER OF THE DAY

I will forget my shame and shall not remember my reproach any more, for God Almighty will bless me beyond any shame, pain, failure and reproach. I believe this because the Bible says God cannot lie. I pray in the name of Jesus Christ, with much love and thanksgiving. Amen!

SCRIPTURE OF THE DAY

Fear not; for thou shalt not be ashamed: neither be thou confounded; for thou shalt not be put to shame: for thou shalt forget the shame of thy youth, and shalt not remember the reproach of thy widowhood any more.

--Isaiah 54:4

TODAY'S WORD OF WISDOM

Some men see things as they are and say, "Why?" I dream of things that never were and say, "Why not?"

--George Bernard Shaw

DAY 76

PRAYER OF THE DAY

Oh Lord, take me from where I am now and lead me to where you want me to be. Lord, anoint me for favor in every area of life. I pray in the name of Jesus Christ, with much love and thanksgiving. Amen!

SCRIPTURE OF THE DAY

For I know the thoughts that I think toward you, saith the Lord, thoughts of peace, and not of evil, to give you an expected end.

--Jeremiah 29:11

TODAY'S WORD OF WISDOM

Without leaps of imagination, or dreaming, we lose the excitement of possibilities. Dreaming, after all, is a form of planning.

--Gloria Steinem

DAY 77

PRAYER OF THE DAY

Lord, let your goodness and mercy follow me every day and every second of my life. I pray in the name of Jesus Christ, with much love and thanksgiving. Amen!

SCRIPTURE OF THE DAY

Surely goodness and mercy shall follow me all the days of my life: and I will dwell in the house of the Lord forever.

--Psalm 23:6

TODAY'S WORD OF WISDOM

Dream no small dreams for they have no power to move the hearts of men.

--Johann Wolfgang von Goethe

DAY 78

PRAYER OF THE DAY

Lord, as you prospered Joseph in the land of Egypt, be with me in every area of my interest, and whatever I lay my hands on shall prosper. I pray in the name of Jesus Christ, with much love and thanksgiving. Amen!

SCRIPTURE OF THE DAY

The keeper of the prison looked not to anything that was under his hand; because the Lord was with him, and that which he did, the Lord made it to prosper.

--Genesis 39:23

TODAY'S WORD OF WISDOM

I have learned, that if one advances confidently in the direction of his dreams, and endeavors to live the life he has imagined, he will meet with a success unexpected in common hours.

--Henry David Thoreau

DAY 79

PRAYER OF THE DAY

Lord, I don't want to waste my time any longer. Please show me your plan for my life. I pray in the name of Jesus Christ, with much love and thanksgiving. Amen!

SCRIPTURE OF THE DAY

And I will make of thee a great nation, and I will bless thee, and make thy name great; and thou shalt be a blessing.

--Genesis 12:2

TODAY'S WORD OF WISDOM

Dreams are the touchstones of our character.

--Henry David Thoreau

DAY 80

PRAYER OF THE DAY

Lord, your Word says all things are mine. I claim my financial freedom today. I pray in the name of Jesus Christ, with much love and thanksgiving. Amen!

SCRIPTURE OF THE DAY

And again, the Lord knoweth the thoughts of the wise, that they are vain. Therefore let no man glory in men. For all things are yours.

--I Corinthians 3:20-21

TODAY'S WORD OF WISDOM

I think we dream so we don't have to be apart so long. If we're in each other's dreams, we can be together all the time.

--Hobbes

DAY 81

PRAYER OF THE DAY

I know that anointing makes the difference. Today, oh Lord, I receive anointing to live a better life. I pray in the name of Jesus Christ, with much love and thanksgiving. Amen!

SCRIPTURE OF THE DAY

And the Spirit of the Lord will come upon thee, and thou shalt prophesy with them, and shalt be turned into another man.

--I Samuel 10:6

TODAY'S WORD OF WISDOM

No one should negotiate their dreams. Dreams must be free to flee and fly high. No government, no legislature, has a right to limit your dreams. You should never agree to surrender your dreams.

--Jesse Jackson

DAY 82

PRAYER OF THE DAY

Today, oh God, re-arrange my life for breakthroughs. I pray in the name of Jesus Christ, with much love and thanksgiving. Amen!

SCRIPTURE OF THE DAY

For I will pour water upon him that is thirsty, and floods upon the dry ground: I will pour my spirit upon thy seed, and my blessing upon thy offspring: And they shall spring up as among the grass, as willows by the water courses.

--Isaiah 44:3-4

TODAY'S WORD OF WISDOM

Imagine all the people living life in peace. You may say I'm a dreamer, but I'm not the only one. I hope someday you'll join us, and the world will live as one.

--John Lennon

DAY 83

PRAYER OF THE DAY

Today, oh Lord, I claim a better job and better business ideas that will surprise everyone around me. I pray in the name of Jesus Christ, with much love and thanksgiving. Amen!

SCRIPTURE OF THE DAY

Blessed shalt thou be in the city, and blessed shalt thou be in the field. Blessed shall be the fruit of thy body, and the fruit of thy ground, and the fruit of thy cattle, the increase of thy kine, and the flocks of thy sheep.

--Deuteronomy 28:3-4

TODAY'S WORD OF WISDOM

The most pitiful among men is he who turns his dreams into silver and gold.

--Kahlil Gibran

DAY 84

PRAYER OF THE DAY

I have tried for many years, and all my efforts could not help me.
But this year, oh Lord, teach me how to wait upon you. Save me,
rescue me from this so called busy schedule. Please lead me and
show me how to wait. I pray in the name of Jesus Christ, with
much love and thanksgiving. Amen!

SCRIPTURE OF THE DAY

Even the youths shall faint and be weary, and the young men shall
utterly fall: But they that wait upon the Lord shall renew their
strength; they shall mount up with wings as eagles; they shall run,
and not be weary; and they shall walk, and not faint.

--Isaiah 40:30-31

TODAY'S WORD OF WISDOM

If a little dreaming is dangerous, the cure for it is not to dream less
but to dream more, to dream all the time.

--Marcel Proust

DAY 85

PRAYER OF THE DAY

Create in me a clean heart, oh God; and renew a right spirit within me. Teach me and help me to do what is right. I pray in the name of Jesus Christ, with much love and thanksgiving. Amen!

SCRIPTURE OF THE DAY

A new heart also will I give you, and a new spirit will I put within you: and I will take away the stony heart out of your flesh, and I will give you a heart of flesh. And I will put my spirit within you, and cause you to walk in my statutes, and ye shall keep my judgments, and do them.

--Ezekiel 36:26-27

TODAY'S WORD OF WISDOM

No person has the right to rain on your dreams.

--Marian Wright Edelman

DAY 86

PRAYER OF THE DAY

Continue your loving-kindness unto me oh Lord, and satisfy my soul with riches and good health. I pray in the name of Jesus Christ, with much love and thanksgiving. Amen!

SCRIPTURE OF THE DAY

O continue thy lovingkindness unto them that know thee; and thy righteousness to the upright in heart.

--Psalm 36:10

TODAY'S WORD OF WISDOM

Twenty years from now you will be more disappointed by the things that you didn't do than by the ones you did do. So throw off the bowlines. Sail away from the safe harbor. Catch the trade winds in your sails. Explore. Dream. Discover.

--Mark Twain

DAY 87

PRAYER OF THE DAY

Look upon me, oh God, and be merciful unto me, as you always do unto those who love your name. I pray in the name of Jesus Christ, with much love and thanksgiving. Amen!

SCRIPTURE OF THE DAY

Look thou upon me, and be merciful unto me, as thou usest to do unto those that love thy name.

--Psalm 119:132

TODAY'S WORD OF WISDOM

If you lose hope, somehow you lose the vitality that keeps life moving, you lose that courage to be, that quality that helps you go on in spite of it all. And so today I still have a dream.

--Martin Luther King Jr.

DAY 88

PRAYER OF THE DAY

Lead me, direct me and order my steps, oh Lord, so I will not miss my way in life. I pray in the name of Jesus Christ, with much love and thanksgiving. Amen!

SCRIPTURE OF THE DAY

Order my steps in thy word: and let not any iniquity have dominion over me.

--Psalm 119:133

TODAY'S WORD OF WISDOM

If growing up is the process of creating ideas and dreams about what life should be, then maturity is letting go again.

--Mary Beth Danielson

DAY 89

PRAYER OF THE DAY

Turn away my reproach, oh God. Bless me with miracles and restore me to what you have created me to be. I pray in the name of Jesus Christ, with much love and thanksgiving. Amen!

SCRIPTURE OF THE DAY

Turn away my reproach which I fear: for thy judgments are good. Behold, I have longed after thy precepts: quicken me in thy righteousness.

--Psalm 119:39-40

TODAY'S WORD OF WISDOM

The best love affairs are those we never had.

--Norman Lindsay

DAY 90

PRAYER OF THE DAY

Your Word says, there is nothing too hard for you. Today, oh Lord, turn my situations around for the better and let my life become a testimony to others. I pray in the name of Jesus Christ, with much love and thanksgiving. Amen!

SCRIPTURE OF THE DAY

Behold, I am the Lord, the God of all flesh: is there anything to hard for me?.

--Jeremiah 32:27

TODAY'S WORD OF WISDOM

Judge your natural character by what you do in your dreams.

--Ralph Waldo Emerson

$\mathcal{T}$ESTIMONIES

What People Around the World Are Saying About Prayer of the Day

I read the *Prayer of the Day* every day before I commence my daily activities. It is assuring, spiritual and fulfilling. It empowers me for the day's journey. I always look forward to reading it daily. Thank you
------ Yinka

I have really benefited from all your mails and I feel I should commend the power of the love of God in you. *The Prayer of the Day* is a good vision and I pray for its continuity of existence. It calls for absolute reliance and total dependence on God for a glorious Christian life in this present dispensation. May God renew your strength, Amen.
------ Shade

Your ministry has been a blessing not to me alone, but, I believe, to everyone who takes time to read *The Prayer of the Day* daily.
------- Bose

Your prayers have really been an uplifting experience and blessing in my life, as well as the lives of my family and others.
------- Jenkins

Glory and praise be to God! Thank you for your daily prayer devotions, and thank you for lifting me in prayer.
------- Betty

Thank you for keeping me on your list! *The Prayer of the Day* energizes me every morning. I really need that and this has really helped me tremendously!
------- Grace

I thank God Almighty for your life and ministry, which has brought about joy, happiness and great things in my life. Each day I look forward to opening my mail because I know I will definitely find the spiritual and physical vitamin I need to help me carry on and obtain my blessing of the day. I now have a job - and not just any job - but the type I want, which is by God's grace. As you have been a blessing in my life and the lives of thousands by bringing hope and finally testimonies, God in his infinite mercy will continue to be your strength in the name of Jesus Christ, Amen.
------- Jane

I just want to say thanks for your daily dose of God's word and blessings. You hit the nail right on the head. Please continue to send me those words. Sometimes people pray but don't know how to pray. The words you send tell me exactly what to pray for. Thank you, and may God continue to bless you and your family.
------ Marie

I most often wonder and have finally come to the conclusion that God truly works wonders. The Spirit with which the Word of God is written is inspired by God. Every day that I receive and read this daily nugget, especially the prayers, the words always reflect the situation of my mind. This has happened not once, not twice, but several times, and I have had to forward *The Prayer of the Day* to a friend and colleague of mine.
------ Williams

Thank you very much for your inspirational words of encouragement. Surely I will inform you of my testimony when it manifests, and we shall all glorify God Almighty. It's beautiful to know that somewhere, someone really cares. God bless.
------ Vivian

I just wanted to say thank you for my *Prayer of the Day* e-mail each morning! I look forward to receiving it and I am always so blessed by it. It is so amazing that each prayer fits each day so perfectly! May you and your ministry be forever blessed!
------ Watts-Reeves

101

I just want to let you know that *The Prayer of the Day* has truly been a blessing in my life. It truly is a spiritual vitamin and I have been blessed since I began reading it. I will make sure to pass it on so others can be blessed. Thank you for following the Lord and providing this to people.
------- Seun James

Your program has been a blessing to me and I know it will equally bless many. It has indeed been the spiritual vitamin that blesses my soul daily. I am therefore writing to congratulate you and encourage you to please continue with the daily message. You can never know how many people the Lord is using you to touch on a daily basis. God the rewarder of those who diligently seek Him and the rewarder of those who seek the good of others will surely reward you, sir. Continue to enjoy the goodness of the Lord in your life, my brother.
------- Pastor Oluwaluyi

There is such a heavy anointing on your life and the work that you're doing for the Lord. How do I know? I was able to feel it when I opened the e-mail. God bless you, your family and your ministry.
------- Oliver

To read more testimonies and what people all around the world are saying about Prayer of The Day, visit our website at www.glovimonline.org

I would love to hear from you also. You may send your testimony or prayer request to:

Glovim Publications
Global Vision Ministries Inc.
1096 Bethsaida Road
Riverdale, GA 30296 USA.
Or via email:
information@glovimonline.org

ABOUT THE AUTHOR

Tim Atunnise is the senior pastor of Global Vision Ministries in Atlanta, Ga. He was called into ministry at the age of 23 as a pastor, prophet and dynamic teacher of the Word. Atunnise believes that you must discover the anointing and power of God within you, realize that you have everything you need to fulfill your God-given destiny, and stand on God's promises, protecting them at all costs with power of prayer.

Tim Atunnise is a highly sought-after counselor, business consultant and entrepreneurial trainer. This is a story of what is possible for those who love God and are called according to His purpose (Romans 8:28). Atunnise spent an impoverished childhood in Nigeria. From his trials and triumphs, you will learn the power of vision, responsibility, integrity and faithfulness. More importantly, you will know beyond a doubt that with God, all things are possible (Matthew 19:26).

$\mathcal{S}$UBSCRIPTION $\mathcal{F}$ORM

Prayer of the day is "Prayer on the Go". The spiritual vitamin to energize your day and nourish your soul. To order "Prayer of the Day" Volume 2 or to order for the entire year subscription, fill and mail in the form below.

Get one year of Prayer of the Day Book Volume (Four books) for just $39.95! Four books for the price of three.

___ Please enter my one-year subscription to Prayer of the Day for $39.95 using the information below.
___ I just want a copy of Prayer of the Day for $12.95 using the information below.
Circle one - Volume I   Volume II

Name _____
(Please print)

Company or
Organization _____

Address _____

City _____ State _____ Zip _____

Tel _____ E-mail _____

[ ] My check or money order for $12.95 is enclosed for a copy of Prayer of the Day.
[ ] My check or money order for $39.95 is enclosed for a year subscription of Prayer of the Day.

To pay by mail send your check or money order with this form to:
Tim Atunnise
c/o Prayer of the Day
5115 King Arthur Lane
Ellenwood, GA 30294
To pay online by paypal using your credit or debit card, visit www.glovimonline.org. [ ] MasterCard [ ] Visa [ ] Amex

For more information about special discounts for bulk purchases and/or discounts on books purchases for distribution in homeless shelters, nursing homes, hospitals, orphanages, etc. contact information@glovimonline.org,